BREAKING THE ICE

All rights reserved. No part of this work may be reproduced or stored in an information retrieval system (other than for purposes of review) without the express permission of the publisher in writing.

The right of G C Burnell to be identified as the author of this work has been asserted by him in accordance with the Copyright, Designs and Patents Act 1988

Copyright © 2017 G C Burnell.

Published by AMORY PUBLISHING

To contact the publisher, in the first instance message them from their website:

www.AmoryPublishing.co.uk

To see details of other books offered by Amory Publishing:

www.AmoryPublishing.co.uk

CONTENTS

SECTION I

Article 1.1	7
Article 1.2	13
Article 1.3	17
Article 1.4	35
Article 1.5	41
Article 1.6	43
Article 1.7	49
Article 1.8	53
Article 1.9	57

SECTION II

Fragments of Autobiography	63

SECTION III

Article 3.1	97
Article 3.2	101
Article 3.3	107
Article 3.4	109
Article 3.5	111
Article 3.6	115
Article 3.7	119
Article 3.8	121
Article 3.9	125
Article 3.10	129
Article 3.11	133
Article 3.12	137

SECTION I

I wrote several introductions to this section, none of which I liked very much and, after all, it is easy to tell roughly what is included by looking at the contents page – so have decided instead to get straight away on to the nitty-gritty!

Article 1

Have The Power Of A Roman Army Centurion – Give Yourself 100 Chances Of Success (In Getting V Good Conversations Out Of Nothing)

10 X 10 Must Do's.

(It might take you up to 4 months to get up to this situation if you're nowhere near yet.)

1) Get info on 10 types of job.

2) Get info on 10 industries (eg banking, insurance and building are 3 industries).

3) Know of/about 10 local pubs (know ones that have discos/karaokes/live groups/quizzes [1 or 2 of each])

4) Know something about 10 bands/singers (well known nationally).

5) You would ideally have seen at least 10 films in the last 4 months, and read something about them too eg reviews.

6) Know something about 10 local firms (quite large size preferably).

7) Also within the last 4 months, you would ideally have bought at least 10 albums/CDs.

8) Know something about (and have tried) 10 popular drinks.

9) Know something about 10 interests/hobbies (and be a 'participant' of at least 2).

10) Know something about 10 local clubs (i.e. name of club, what they do, where they meet, day of week, etc) – and be a member of at least 2.

These are the 100 (10 x 10) imperatives.

Comment

Many of these 'conversation points' may be chosen as an opening gambit to start a conversation with a (relative) stranger. An example is to say something about what is on the jukebox, if you're in a pub, for instance.

As regards that, of course, a very good investment is to put a few records on the jukebox yourself. Obviously you can choose to put on records that you know something about (or the band or singer) and that you can make intelligent comments about. Why leave things like this to chance?

Another similar example. Perhaps it is a bit warm – you can say something like "Wow, it's a bit warm, isn't it? – a bit too warm to go to the pictures really – I went and saw that film (such and such) this afternoon."

And if you're either good at talking about films you've seen, or if as well you've read a review about it, like I suggested, you're in! – you'll come across as a lot more interesting than someone who starts saying something about what's happening in Coronation Street at the moment.

(And you don't really have to have seen that film that afternoon – it may have been a week or so before – but who's to know? Just as long as it's actually still showing at the cinema.)

And of course a lot of the things I've mentioned in the above article are very useful during a 15 minute 'initial encounter', if you're granted it.

For example, very likely the person will tell you what they do for a living.

In most towns, there are only a few major employers (these are of course the ones you will have researched). If your conversation partner happens to work for one of those you'll really be able to impress him/her, won't you? Failing that, you may have researched the industry they work in, or failing that the type of job – so you'll effectively have 3 bites of the cherry.

Going back to doing the research on companies.

On these grounds there's a lot to be said for buying a few shares in 3 or 4 of your local companies. You'd be surprised. Someone with maybe just £100 of shares (or less) will often be given an enormous amount of information about a company (in the Chairman's report, for instance) – far more, usually, than a loyal employee who's worked for the firm for 20 years! If you're going to spend £500 on shares anyway…

Article 1.2

On Preparation

When we are socialising – perhaps having a few drinks with friends down the pub, or (for the more posh) at a dinner party, surely we are 'giving a performance' of some sort – isn't that true?

And it has occurred to me that whereas everyone agrees that it is important for us all to have friendships or relationships of some sort – maybe it is this 'performance aspect' that is the really important thing (or at least as important as the friendship or relationship itself).

Following on from this... when we think of people who very obviously 'give performances' as part of their job – actors and actresses, singers, comedians, or even managers who have to give a lot of presentations – what is always required?

<u>Answer</u>: A lot of preparation. An actor with anything other than a very minor role wouldn't dream of going on stage without hours of preparation – he must get those lines word perfect. A comedian, too – although he may be very proud of his ad-libbing, you can bet nine-tenths of his act will be very well rehearsed. Singers too would have prepared well, and even that manager with her 20 minute speech to give.

Each would totally humiliate themselves if they tried to do these things without any preparation.

And it just strikes me that, bearing in mind what I said earlier – that we can consider when we are socialising as a 'performance' – that hardly any of us do nearly enough preparation for them.

I suppose the trouble is, after 8 hours of quite likely soul-destroying, boring work, they just want to go out and enjoy themselves – and they certainly haven't got time for an hour or so of reading a day, and other types of preparation.

Even worse, maybe they haven't even got the energy for going out very often, but instead slump in front of the TV for 5 hours most evenings.

Incidentally, if you do find time for a reasonable amount of reading, further on in this book you will come across recommendations for the sort of thing it is a good idea, in my view, to read about.

Moving on to talk about the 'performance' aspect.

Although socialising in a group may be thought of as 'a performance' I think it is good for us to be involved with some sort of hobby or interest that involves giving performances.

In article 1.3 I suggest that for a lot of us 'thinking of ourselves as a bit of a comedian' and, in fact, 'training as if we are going to be a comic', is probably one of the best options whereby we can fulfil this.

Article 1.3

Why Not Train Like A Comedian?

In the last article, I said that it would be a good idea if we chose a hobby or interest that involved 'giving performances'. One might think possibly joining a drama group, or as an alternative, taking up a musical instrument might be good. But I'm going to start off in this article – with rather a long preamble – saying why, in my view, drama or playing music isn't the best option for a lot of people.

I personally feel that taking up acting would be out of the question for me – I've always known that, really, because I just don't have the kind of memory that would enable me to learn lines easily. It would be just about impossible for me to learn anything but a very small part.

Nevertheless, for the same reason that I recommend reading a book or two on art in a later article, I bought a book on acting a few weeks ago, and have been reading that. The book is called '*Respect for acting*', and it's by Uta Hagan.

It's actually about 'Method acting' in particular – that's Ms Hagan's speciality.

Although I'm enjoying reading it, and don't regret buying it at all, it's becoming more and more clear to me that for all sorts of reasons, besides the inability I would have to memorise lines, I could never have been an actor.

For example, there's something called 'substitution', which an upcoming actor/actress has to master. I'll try and explain briefly what this is.

When you are playing a part in a play, and doing it well, you are expected to 'live' your character. That is, show the emotions etc that the person (character) in the play would be expected to have in whatever circumstances there are.

Not surprisingly, I suppose, this is apparently one of the most difficult things actors have to do. It doesn't just happen that if you are pretending to be someone in a play, you have the feelings/emotions that person would be expected to have at any time.

This is where you have to use the process called substitution.

Suppose at a particular point in a play, your character must show a certain kind of fear – an example given in Uta Hagan's book is from Shakespeare's Othello – the final scene where Othello wants to murder Desdemona.

Then – Uta Hagan says – the actress playing Desdemona must think back to a time in her life when she felt a similar emotion. It is unlikely that her life would ever have been threatened in quite a similar way to Desdemona, but it is suggested that the emotion she might have felt before having surgery, or even sitting in a dentist's reception room before having a tooth extracted, might be an equivalent feeling.

So, in other words, you are supposed to think back to an appropriate experience like that, and 're-manufacture' the feeling.

And this process keeps on happening when you're playing a role in a play, apparently. Obviously you will be called on to show lots of different emotions in the course of playing a major character in a play, and therefore you need to make many substitutions – thinking back to times in your life when you would have felt similarly, and re-manufacturing that feeling 'from your memory', as it were.

And I know that this is another thing that would be absolutely impossible for me to do. It's just that I have a very strong defensive system, if you like – which has given me a powerful 'forgetery' in certain cases, which would make it more impossible for me to do this than even to memorise a lot of lines.

And I'm pretty sure that a high percentage of people would find this very difficult too – too difficult really.

What I'm saying is that acting is obviously such a difficult thing to do really well, that I don't think it's the ideal interest or hobby for most of us to choose to be the way to give our 'performances'.

And learning how to play a musical instrument well is also probably beyond many of us – I think you really have to start young (when a child) for that, ideally.

What else is there that involves giving performances, besides acting or music?

Another obvious 'job' that fits is being a stand-up comedian.

Here again, though, to be a very successful stand-up comic – having an audience of 500, maybe more people, and being able to make them laugh very frequently over a period of perhaps one and a half hours – must be a very hard job indeed. I doubt if more than 1 in 1000 could do it really well, even with training.

But I've been thinking about it, and while I'm not going to suggest that many of us actually become stand-up comedians in the sense just given, I do think that to think of ourselves as 'a comedian' is probably the best way most of us can fulfil this need of 'giving performances' – but not in front of 500 people, in most cases.

Let me explain.

When you see the 'lonely hearts' columns in newspapers, it is very common for people to say they are looking for someone with 'a good sense of humour' – I believe the abbreviation gsoh is often used.

It's fairly universal, I think, that people want to go out with others with a sense of humour.

And hardly anyone is willing to admit that they don't have one, are they? – Then why not capitalise on it more than most people do?

I said in Article 1.2, that ideally we needed to be able to give a lot of 'preparation time' to be able to live life to the full. As I write this, I'm beginning to see why we really do need a lot of time to do what we must do.

As I said, think of yourself as a comedian – rather than, say, an accounts clerk, or a computer programmer, or whatever.

And take it seriously (no pun intended!).

That is to say, although I'm not going to suggest (in most cases) that you set yourself up professionally as a stand-up comic, *imagine* that you are.

So – buy books on being a stand-up comic. (I've read *'Successful stand up comedy'* by Gene Perret, for instance, and it's an extremely good book.)

Spend maybe an hour and a half a day for three months preparing yourself for this 'role' (of being a comedian). Besides reading books like the above-mentioned, read joke books (and be selective when you read these). Only try to learn the jokes you find really funny.

Put the jokes you've selected on tape maybe, and play the tape over and over again – spend perhaps half an hour of your hour and a half each day doing this.

Although most of us aren't going to want (or at any rate, be able to succeed with), an audience of 500 people who have paid £20, and who are going to get very annoyed if we don't make them laugh very frequently, we are going to want an audience of some kind, aren't we?

Okay, then, join some clubs. Not comedy clubs, I don't mean, but any sort of club. If you are interested in photography, join a photography club. Or a chess club. Whatever. In fact, preferably join 2 or 3 clubs perhaps.

And begin to think of yourself as the 'resident comedian'. You then have your audience.

(You may not even need to do this – if you are a regular at a certain pub, just simply carry on doing that, but become funnier – or similarly if you regularly drink with a certain group of people – the same.)

In this book I've read ('*Successful stand-up comedy*'), there is a bit where a comedian was told he was going to have an audience (it was a kind of convention) of psychiatrists – but it turned out the comedian's agent had got it wrong – the audience were actually chiropractors. The comedian had naturally prepared lots of jokes relating to psychiatry, but these turned out to be unsuitable.

What this is saying, of course, is that your jokes need to be *relevant.*

If you're joining a photographic club, for instance, you mainly need jokes relating to photographers and photography. Probably you will be able to find quite a few jokes relating to photography on the internet, if you know how to use the search engines competently. (I doubt if any of the joke books you get from Smiths will have lots of jokes on photography.)

One thing to note – it's in the preface in a

book of jokes I bought recently – (it says) "In conversation, try to tell jokes which 'arise' from the subject being discussed." That is, of course, by far the best approach you can adopt. I don't recommend, usually, suddenly saying out of the blue, "Does anyone know any jokes – I know a few?"

It also says in this book "Remember that the secret of being a good teller of jokes lies as much in the way you tell it as in the joke itself".

Therefore, obviously you need to practice, rehearse – like an actor I suppose – it is all quite hard work, I agree, but I'm sure the rewards are worth it.

So – we have found our **therapeutic** solution to our need to give performances that we were looking for – learning and telling jokes. But the benefits go deeper than this. Gene Perret (author of *"Successful Stand-Up Comedy"*) writes 'Much humour is revenge. It's a way of getting even with the world for injustices,' (or, in other words, for things that make us angry) – therefore this is another reason why it is very therapeutic. So we now have two reasons why learning and telling jokes is extremely good for us.

Since writing (most of) this article I have been reading 2 or 3 other 'how to' books on stand-up comedy – for example, *"Getting the joke"* by Oliver Double, *"Teach yourself stand-up comedy"* by Logan Murray and *"Zen and the art of stand-up comedy"* by Jay Sankey. I thought they were all excellent books, though completely different from each other. However, there was one thing they all had in common which they didn't share with *"Successful Stand-up Comedy"* by Gene Perret.

This 'thing' or attitude that the writers of the above-mentioned 3 books have in common is the belief that comedians should all write their own material. Whereas Gene Perret, who is a comedy writer, not a performer, obviously has the view that you have comedy writers, and comedy performers, and they form teams (each one needs the other).

I may be wrong, but I almost have the impression that these 3 other comedians and authors very much look down on comedians who can't write their own material.

I *can* see where they're coming from. They're saying that being a comedian is about expressing yourself very personally – it's giving your own personal 'take' on the world – and how can you be doing that if the writer is a different person?

That may be so, but I can't help thinking that the *talents* of being a comedy writer and comedy performer are entirely different. I can't help but imagine that you might have 20 excellent comedy writers, and 20 excellent comedy performers, and perhaps only 1 of those 40 people would be a great writer *and* performer.

So I tend to be on Gene Perret's side here, and think that comedy is losing out a lot by seemingly insisting (these days) that the performer and writer should be the same person.

I realise that the price a potential performer might pay for, say, a 5 minute comedy routine, to a professional writer would be very considerable (if the writer was any good). And this would be out of the range of a wannabe comedian who had given up his job, hoping to make it on the comedy club circuit, before becoming very successful. But that is surely not how this career should be approached, in any case.

Moving on now, but still to something slightly related.

Have you noticed when celebrities are interviewed on TV, eg by Piers Morgan, or Alan Titchmarsh, or - well, by any of the chat show hosts – their conversation is nearly always quite scintillating? – compared to, say, the average conversation you might overhear, or be part of, in a pub, for instance. Have you ever wondered if it's only actors and actresses (and talk show hosts) who can talk like that?

Well, of course, it's all rehearsed.

If they don't actually do a rehearsed performance, I'm sure the interviewees know more or less precisely what questions are going to be asked, and spend a lot of time rehearsing what they are going to say.

There's no reason why you or I shouldn't do the same thing, is there?

Going back to being a comedian – of course all professional comedians have to have (at least one) 'spiel' – their performance.

Why don't we do the same?

Not made up (mostly) of jokes, but this is what I've been thinking…

They say everyone has a book in them, don't they?

Why don't you (I'm suggesting) make up a book consisting of two parts. For the first part, you think of, and write down, all the interesting experiences you've had in your life – everything that you don't mind people knowing about, that is.

It can be in chronological order – that might be simplest, but it doesn't really matter. Some of the experiences probably will be amusing, but there's all sorts of ways that an experience can be 'interesting' to others (depending on who it is).

Write in a conversational tone, and then improve it – the first draft of virtually anything a writer writes is usually then 'polished' – the second or third drafts are almost always a considerable improvement.

So – you end up with a document of considerable length, hopefully – if you write 2 or 3 pages a day it'll soon build up to a reasonable size – maybe 40 or 50 different experiences in your life.

Then I suggest you put it on tape, but don't show it to anyone – not even your partner, if you have one.

For the second part of this book, you will get your material mainly from reading biographies, I would suggest. Obviously the biographies (or autobiographies) you will want to read will be of your heroes or heroines, or the people you find most interesting, at any rate – maybe sportsmen or women, scientists or writers (past or present) – whatever.

Just about all biographies or autobiographies contain a lot of what might be called 'anecdotes' – and this is what makes for good conversation.

As you read a biography, you will find a few (anecdotes) that are – in your view – much more interesting/amusing than the rest of it.

Even if in each biography/autobiography you read, you only find on average 5 anecdotes that you find extremely interesting or amusing, and you write them down (into your book), you will soon have quite a collection of the most noteworthy experiences of your favourite well known people, even if you only spend a quarter of an hour or half an hour each day reading biographies (which I'm suggesting you do).

Your book will therefore grow, perhaps by 5 – 10 pages every time you complete a biography. So – of course you will have the whole book (both parts) on tape, and you can play it back to yourself regularly, and learn it well – learn it better than any book you've learnt before, I would suggest. In a sense, it is your most important book. But I will repeat, it is not for anyone else to read but you.

You will find that when you're in a conversation, someone will say something that reminds you of something that is in your book, and that is relevant. Often you'll be able to tell your 'story', which you may even have rehearsed.

You probably won't be quite as polished as the 'professional conversationalists' (celebrity actors and actresses etc) you see on talk shows – but I guarantee you'll come across a great deal better than previously – assuming you don't already do something like this.

Article 1.4

Your Choice Of Reading – To Improve Conversation Skills

In my opinion, probably the most important reason for reading is to improve your conversation skills. Therefore your choice of reading material should, above all else, reflect this aim. You should have a fairly general knowledge over a wide range of subjects, but I'm not talking about the sort of 'general knowledge' that helps you to be good at quizzes, really.

The best way to explain what I mean is to tell you what I did this morning. These ideas are new to me, as well as possibly you. As I write this I am not nearly as widely read as I would like to be, on a wide range of subjects.

In other words, I'm not writing as an 'expert' as such, but simply as someone with a few ideas, which I'm convinced are pretty okay.

So, I went into a bookshop – not a massive one, but a reasonably sized one – with a view to choosing books, up to about 15 I had in mind, specifically to improve my knowledge in subjects I, as yet, know very little about, but would like to know more.

I literally went round all the departments – the subject headings were displayed at the top of the shelves containing those books, of course. For each subject heading I thought "do I want to know anything about that?" – sometimes I decided "no, not really", and other times it was "yes, it would be a good idea to know a little in that area."

One subject which I decided I'd like to know a little about is art.

I am a pretty bad artist actually – but, funnily enough, one of the best relationships I had was with a professional artist. (She never got to find out how bad at art I was, because I never showed her.) But as I was walking round this bookshop this morning, I thought that it would be nice to know just a little bit about art.

It's quite likely some of the people you meet will have a pretty keen interest in art, and even if you only chose one book on the subject to read and study, it would mean you could probably impress those people who may have an art degree, say, more than 95% of the non-artists he or she will meet.

So I looked through the shelves containing books on art. Most of them were inappropriate – it would be little use to me to choose a book containing reproductions of one famous artist's 100 most well known paintings, for instance – what would I be able to say about that? I did not want too big a book either – as I said, art is not one of my specialist subjects – and I didn't want to wade through a 500 page book.

In the end, the one that seemed most promising seemed to me to be *"Teach yourself art history"* by Grant Pooke and Graham Whitham. It was a little larger than I would have liked, but I thought it the best of what was available for what I needed.

I also thought later, after leaving the bookshop, that it might be an idea to buy just one other book on the subject of art. A more specialised one.

About a week ago I was in a group of people, but not really interested in the conversation. I detached myself and looked through the bookshelf in the room. The books were on many subjects, but one on Impressionism caught my eye. I spent half an hour reading through the introduction to the book. Really I found it very interesting, so this has given me the idea, that as well as the general book on art, I might also get a specialised book – quite possibly on Impressionism. But it really wouldn't matter (the exact subject), as long as I found it quite interesting. (And I would absolutely stick to just the one specialised book on art.)

The idea would be that if I found myself with an artist, or someone very interested in art, if the conversation got onto that, first of all I would be able to make a few intelligent comments (and not feel a complete dunce), because of the general book I had read. And then at some point I might say something like "I'm afraid I'm not very well up on art, though I did read a book on Impressionism once and found it quite interesting."

This would mean that, for a while, you could maybe talk more or less on equal terms with your conversation partner on *their* subject, which they would probably find quite impressive.

You should not overdo it though – you do not want to come across as more knowledgeable than them on their ground – that would not go down well at all.

[And it would be possible – there are always a lot of options in degree courses, and you never do them all. It is quite possible (using the above example) someone with a degree in art may have avoided all the options on Impressionism – and you, with your knowledge gleaned from just one book, could find you know more than him or her on that one particular area of art. If anything like that happens you should change the subject very quickly.]

I'm not going to tell you all the dozen books I found that I thought it would be good to invest in as soon as possible – I'm not giving all my secrets away! But you get the general idea.

Apart from what I've said above, I feel that we should have probably about 2 (and no more than 3) specialist subjects about which we should know quite a bit.

I'm not going to say much about how to approach making some area a specialist subject except that I think that for relaxation, listening to music is just about the best thing for most people. (Speaking personally, much better than watching television, for instance.) Since I also think that quite a lot of time should be allocated for 'relaxation', this would mean that you would probably be spending a lot of time listening to music. Therefore it would make sense to make music (whatever type of music you like best), one of your 'specialist areas'. Articles 1.5 and 1.6 have something to say about that.

Article 1.5

Music (1)

Idea 1) Make a deliberate effort to listen to as many different types of music as possible, to see what suits you best. It is quite likely that the types of music you find in the top 100 – what nearly everyone buys nearly every time – aren't what will be best for you.

Idea 2) Read about music too for a significant amount of time (relative to how much time you spend listening to it). I don't necessarily mean about the *theory*, but for instance, biographies of pop stars, bands, composers. When I started doing this my enjoyment of the music increased immensely. (And as a side-effect one's conversation skills are enhanced considerably.)

Idea/recommendation 3) If possible, be a 'participant' in some respect too – either singing or playing an instrument.

Article 1.6

Music (2)

This article is for those who decide to follow my recommendation at the end of article 1.4 – to make music (perhaps a couple of genres of music that particularly appeal to you) one of your specialist subjects. You will really also need access to the internet to do the researching that I'm going to suggest in the following paragraphs.

I mentioned in the last article about reading biographies of pop stars, bands, composers – musicians. A high percentage of my reading related to music is doing this.

The online bookshop Amazon.co.uk is an amazing tool for the research one needs to do. I suggest you type into the search box things like: 'biographies musicians'; 'biographies pop music'; 'biographies rock music'; 'biographies composers' – you get the idea.

On each of these, loads of results will come up. I suggest you spend half an hour or so searching through each one you want to try (for instance 'biographies composers' will be mainly for those who like classical music). Don't just look at the first 10 results (as many people do) – the book you will most want may well be in the 200s!

The next thing I was going to recommend was to acquire perhaps a couple of books in the *Rough Guides to Music* series. They published quite a few, for instance *Rough Guide to Rock, Rough Guide to Opera, Rough Guide to Jazz, Rough Guide to Soul and R&B* etc. The advantage of these is that they typically have about a two page biography of the artists relating to each genre – ideal for researching a significant number of the artists we have CDs of (if we have a sizeable collection).

However – although I acquired a few of these books a couple of years ago, when I looked them up just recently I saw that a lot of books in the series are being taken out of print.

So we must find alternatives.

The main alternative – to obtain brief biographies on artists – is to use Wikipedia (wikipedia.org). Type into the search box *music 'artist's name'*.

There are two main advantages that using Wikipedia has over the books. Firstly, it is much more up to date than books can ever hope to be. If an artist has released a single 2 weeks ago, details will probably be on the Wikipedia entry – entries are normally updated every few days. Another example relates to the compilation album (series) "*Now that's what I call music*". (I have found that playing the latest one of these quite frequently is the best way of keeping up with the latest in chart music without going to the expense of buying lots of individual albums in the top 50.) You will find that virtually all the artists represented in the latest (double) album in this series will have an entry in Wikipedia, even though some of them will only have burst on the scene within the last few months.

Secondly, the books have to be very selective about who they include, simply because of availability of space. For instance, the "*Rough Guide to Soul and R&B*" has about 330 artists represented, whereas I believe there are many more than this who have made a name for themselves. On the other hand virtually all the artists who have made a name for themselves have entries in Wikipedia.

For these reasons many more people use the internet than the books, and I think that's why the books – like the Rough guides mentioned – are going out of print. However I think the quality of the writing is usually better in the books.

By the way, for those who would prefer books, an interesting experiment is to type into the search box on Amazon *"music type" guides.* I have tried this with 'jazz', 'opera', 'soul music', 'R&B music… and they all produce interesting results, including some possible alternatives to the Rough Music guides – for instance the *'All Music guide to Rock (& pop and soul)* by Vladimir Bogdanov and others, which is all of 1300 pages.

I am going to recommend one more book. It is with a bit of a sense of apprehension that I do this because it really is an unconventional thing to do in the circumstances. That is because the book has a different 'market' from this course. Firstly, it is very much written for musicians. Secondly it really seems to be specifically aimed at the young (whereas this course is for all ages).

Anyway, the book is "*The Guerrilla guide to the music business*" by Sarah Davis and Dave Laing (the book is subtitled 'About the music business by people in the music business').

The reason I'm recommending it is because if you're going to read biographies of musicians, I believe it's a great book for getting you to see what musicians have to go through – in the early years of their career especially. Therefore you will be able to have more 'empathy' with them – if that's the right word – as they relate what happened to them, perhaps in the years just before their career took off.

And, for instance, you will see that most don't have an easy time of it at all. Their pay will typically be *very* low in the early years, or even non-existent. And also it seems that they are called upon these days to not only be singers and musicians, but to know a great deal about technical things as well. It seems to me that a typical member of a band needs to be very competent in electrical matters, and also a whizz at electronic equipment and even computing.

And yet – probably most musicians don't make anything like a living wage (from their music).

This book by Sarah Davis and Dave Laing will certainly drive these facts home, and will probably help you to appreciate more the biographies of these musicians whose career does take off sooner or later (if they are the subject of a biography – obviously).

Incidentally, you'll also learn about the roles of other people in the music business besides musicians – for instance managers, agents, promoters and record producers.

Article 1.7

The Movies

I haven't been a great cinema-goer in the past, and even the films I see, I'm not really the sort of 'literary person' who can talk intelligently about the film for fifteen or twenty minutes or something. To be honest, I can quite often talk better about a film after having read a review of it, rather than seeing the film itself. (It may be I'll try and see a few more films in the future.)

But – there are quite a lot of conversations about 'the movies', and if there is someone in a group you want to impress, you can't really do that by remaining completely silent during a conversation about films that can last half an hour or more.

And I have a little project lined up – I haven't fully put it into practice yet - but it should help – and it might appeal to you, too.

There are some excellent books on films going back quite a few decades (the films, not the books) – 'Movies of the 60s', 'Movies of the 70s' – 80s and 90s as well. I don't think I'll go too far back, but I'll probably get the books for the 80s , 90s, and noughties.

In each book, there're about 3 or 4 pages of information about roughly 200 of the most popular (or some criteria of success) films of the decade.*

That still leaves films since 2010,

Personally I think the Time Out annual film guide is the best one on the market (which I have acquired). But there are about 10,000 films reviewed, something like that, and even if you just read the ones since 2010, still too many really – unless you've got bags of time. (Bear in mind that I'm certain most people need to read something like this through several times before they really *learn* it.)

So my plan is this.

In Winchester (which is fairly easy for me to get to) there is a cinema with 2 screens. This is what I want – as you will see, one of the modern multiplexes with about 9 screens would be no good (for these purposes).

I've found out that this cinema advertises each week in the local paper, and that the local library has copies of this paper going back many years.

So – I simply spend a few hours in the library going back through the local paper for the last 'so many years' (back to 2010) and jot down what films have been shown at the cinema. As the most popular ones are shown for 2 weeks or more, that will very probably give me quite a manageable number to study in the Time Out guide.

As I said, I've not fully put this scheme into practice yet – I've been busy writing this book! – but I see no reason at all why it shouldn't help a lot, towards the purposes I need it for.

Reading 3 books and a bit is certainly less time consuming (and cheaper!) than seeing several hundred films, and you never know, doing it may enable you or I to bluff our way through conversations even better than actually seeing the films (quite possibly a long time ago anyway).

Believe it or not, this is another series of books that seems to have been taken out of print since I wrote this article – it seems to be happening to all the best books! As an alternative, I would recommend "1001 movies you must see before you die" – they are in chronological order and it is easy to read the reviews of those produced in, say the last 30 years.

Article 1.8

Another Plus For Stand-Up Comedy

In Article 1.3, I wrote that when we were considering choosing a 'hobby' that involved giving performances, one of the best for many of us was 'training like a comedian' and thinking of ourselves in that light (and I gave the reasons).

Now, suppose we are considering all the 'output' of 'popular culture', and trying to decide what to concentrate on. Obviously the primary consideration will be enjoyment – what do we enjoy the most? But the 'conversation skills' aspect is important too.

And from that point of view in particular, I would like to share with you my ideas. And show you why I feel comedy, again, may hold more promise than other fields (in popular culture) – in this respect anyway.

If you go into an HMV store (HMV is just about the only chain remaining, it seems, that deals in CDs, DVDs etc), there are literally thousands of bands, groups, singers whose albums are displayed. Many, it is true, haven't been in the charts for quite a few years. But there is a market for them all – HMV wouldn't stock them otherwise.

In other words, suppose you were to choose a dozen artists to concentrate on – to buy some of their CDs, maybe read about them a bit. It is absolutely clear that, whoever you chose, you could only 'scratch the surface' out of the thousands that are available.

It is the same with films. Each month "Empire" magazine reviews dozens of new films; perhaps 5 or 6 of these become really popular and are shown in most multiplex cinemas. So over a 5 years spell, say, there are 250 – 300 films that have been shown extensively, in cinemas throughout the country. Again, this is an enormous number and one can be almost overwhelmed – if one tries to know a good deal about a reasonable proportion of them.

But when it comes to comedy it is a different story. If you went into HMV with £150 to spend, you could buy a high percentage of the DVDs by the very well-known stand-up comedians, that are available. Of course there are hundreds of comedians making a good living in the comedy clubs up and down the country, I'm not denying that. But there are relatively few 'mega-stars'. What I am saying is that if you spent £150 on the work of about a dozen of these, and spent 3 or 4 months watching them for, say, an hour a day, you'd have quite a reasonable 'overview' of the 'comedy scene' – at least as regards the big stars, such as you could never get in either music or the movies (with an equivalent investment in time and money).

Article 1.9

A Suggestion About Making Notes On A Book As You're Reading It

If you make notes on the whole book, it will probably slow you down far too much, so that you only have time to read very few books; also you'll end up with more notes on that book than you really want.

On the other hand, if you don't take notes at all, if you're anything like me it'll mean you can't remember a thing about that book, just a few weeks after you've read it.

What is needed is a compromise between these extremes.

When you are in a conversation, you may have an opportunity to say something about a book you're reading or have recently read. This 'opportunity' will not be like an exam question i.e. tell me what you know about a part of the book (the part of the book being *specified by the examiner)*, so that you effectively have to know a lot about the whole book. Instead, the chances are you will be able to say anything you like about any part of the book, within reason. Or, to put it another way – 'tell me what you know about a part of the book (the part of the book *not being specified*)'.

This is a huge advantage, and means that you don't have to know the whole book very well, only some of it.

Suppose that typically, you usually read 10 pages of a book a day for 5 days a week. (This may perhaps take 20 minutes a day.) I would suggest that for the first 3 days (of this '5 day week'), you carry on as before, so you read 30 pages of the book. Then, on the fourth day, choose the one passage out of these 3 that has had the most impact on you – and re-read that. And on the fifth day, make notes on that same passage – not more than 1 page of notes, I would suggest.

So, at the end of the week, you will have read 30 pages, and have 1 page of notes (made from 10 of those pages).

In a month, you will have read 120 pages, and have 4 pages of notes (relating to 40 of those 120 pages). I think that may be enough effort to put into the majority of books. If you usually did that, it would mean that with a 20 minute spell each day, you could 'cover' a dozen books in a year; and you would have enough notes to provide plenty of 'conversational fodder' the whole year through, if you read them frequently.

This would be a much better outcome than the usual one. When in conversation, if someone mentions that they've been reading a book, all you're usually able to get from them about it is whether they liked the book or not – this is what I've found.

....

Going back to what I said about 'that most important book' – that personal book (in Article 1.3) that each of us should have. Remember – I said this:

'(For the first part of this book) you think of, and write down, all the interesting experiences you've had in your life – everything that you don't mind people knowing about, that is.'

Well, as an example of what can be done, here is (part of) my 'personal book' – the part relating to my time at Oxford.

SECTION II

Memoirs of my student days at Oxford University – being religious and involved with the CU

Fragments Of Autobiography

First, there is an introductory note about how I came to be religious (as a student). I was to reject Christianity some time later.

For quite a few years I was an evangelical or 'born again' Christian. I was converted when I first went to university aged 18.

(There is a story to that, in fact. A few months before going to Oxford, as a symptom of stress, I lost my voice – I developed a very distressing stammer which was extremely embarrassing, and made verbal communication very difficult. It lasted throughout my first term there – until the Christmas.

Not surprisingly, most students were not too

friendly – they didn't know how to react. But, true to form, a couple of Christian students were extremely friendly. I have discovered since then that it is a well-practised routine that evangelical Christians often target the most vulnerable people around – and I was certainly very vulnerable at that time.

And those two Christian students were extremely polished performers. They made Christianity sound absolutely marvellous. Some people do have that 'gift'. I am quite sure I wouldn't even have been targeted, let alone responded positively to them, if I hadn't been in such a vulnerable state. But there you are.)

....

It surprises me when I think about it, that I remember that hardly anyone at the college wore jeans. Nearly all the students wore quite smart trousers. I'm quite sure that by that time blue jeans had become the 'uniform' at most universities in the country. But apparently not at Oxford. It probably had something to do with the fact that about two thirds of the students had come from public schools and tended to be very conservative (with both a small and a big 'c').

According to Kate Fox's book "Watching the English", which I thoroughly enjoyed reading a few years ago, 'Freshers week' – the first week new students spend at university, where it is de rigeur to get drunk all the time, talk to as many strangers as possible (the only time in one's life when one does), and have countless second and third year students try to get you to join the clubs and societies they are representatives of – is now a very big deal at universities.

It wasn't quite so established when I became a student, but nevertheless there were still a couple of evenings spent in the JCR (Junior Common Room) where you would be approached by the 'salesmen' for the various college clubs and be expected to try at least something new.

I dutifully took up rowing, but it was a short-lived affair. The rowing club was run by 2 or 3 second or third years students whose keenness seemed to be almost pathological. More about that later.

The 'servants' of the college were called 'scouts'. You would have one come in to clean your room in the morning. Also there would be a few dressed in proper waiters' uniforms, serving you your meals in the dining hall in the evening. I haven't been back to the college for very many years, but it would surprise me if this tradition hasn't completely gone by the wayside. Probably these days it's just like every other educational establishment, serving poor quality food from a self-service counter. (But I stand to be corrected.)

Of course, we soon had to get down to business. I was one of 9 students in the year's intake studying mathematics. There were 2 tutors or 'dons' in the college who specialised in teaching maths – Charlie Caine, who took applied maths subjects (he also taught maths to engineering and science students), who was highly eccentric; and the more conservative Martin Powell, who taught 'pure maths' subjects.

Applied maths meant things like

electromagnetism theory and mechanics (not what car repairers do, but a rather complicated branch of mathematics!). Pure maths was mainly stuff that didn't appear to have much useful purpose back then (but I understand that put-down has since been revoked, and pure mathematicians are now in great demand in many highly useful fields of endeavour, in our modern electronically connected world [the internet etc]).

Anyway, I was saying that Charlie Caine was eccentric. Certainly, he was the first and only teacher I had who, when you got something wrong at a tutorial, would turn to you, stick two fingers up at you, and say "Balls, laddie, balls."

We would have 2 tutorials a week. There would be 2 students with 1 tutor and you were expected to bring up any problems you had had with the week's work. Apart from the 2 tutorials there would also be about half a dozen lectures. Whereas the tutorials were college based, the lectures would be attended by students from all the colleges – they were at the central mathematics building.

Having 2 tutorials and about 6 lectures didn't mean you were only expected to work 8 hours a week, of course. You were expected to attempt to solve a lot of practice problems, both from books, and that lecturers would dish out. Most students were in fact very hard working – 12 hour working days were not at all uncommon amongst students going for very good degrees.

When we turned up at a Charlie Caine tutorial, we would have to make him a very strong coffee. Since this was always the case, he must have been well caffeined up most of the time. But he was a superb mathematician. Apparently when he took his finals at Oxford, he had come in the first 3 or 4 in his year, which is a great achievement (probably the first 20 or so in a year are potential professors, if that's the path they choose).

Through Dan (Hastings), who went from college to college more than most of us, I got to know Andrew, another first year mathematician, from Exeter College. He had ginger hair, a toothy smile and was even more into churchy things than the average member of the God squad. One early afternoon, Dan and I bumped into him in town. We were on our bikes. "I'm desperate," said Andrew, "I've asked these girls round for coffee at 3 this afternoon. There are 8 coming and so far I'm the only man. You can come and give me a hand, can't you?"

Of course, we thought that sounded pretty good, so we agreed. At the appointed time we turned up at Andrew's rooms - which were about 400 years old. He must have repeated his offer to quite a few other men, because there were about 10 male students in the room – but no girls. And no women did come round that afternoon. Not that there would have been any fun and games even if they had. Andrew was a strictly OICCU (Oxford Christian Union) gent through and through and all the talk was going to be about religion anyway.

(And that wasn't the only time we got caught out like that.)

Dan Hastings was to become a Professor at MIT in the USA and became First Scientist in America (some time in the 90s, I think).

When I went to Oxford most colleges were single-sex only. There were far more men's colleges than women's, and overall there was about a 5:1 ratio of men to women. Also there was what was called a town: gown split – people from the university didn't associate hardly at all with the rest of the population of Oxford. The upshot of this was that it was very difficult for male students to find girlfriends. It was very common for male students to do all their 3 years at Oxford without one. In fact it was more or less an accepted situation and the standard 'being in a group of men talking about girls', which occupied a significant amount of time wherever else I lived, right up to my thirties, just didn't happen at Oxford.

I remember, just before my second year, falling for a girl called Jenny. We were both taking part in the mission which St Aldates church organised, for the students to help in, every summer vacation. She was a year above me, very attractive with fair hair, and was studying modern languages. I spent one afternoon (or maybe more) trudging round from house to house with her during this mission. We had to ask the residents if they were interested in Christianity and if they would like to come to one of the many evening group meetings which were held during the fortnight, which were evangelistic in tone and were attended by some church members at the local church, 2 students from St Aldates, and as many 'interested persons' as we could find.

I don't think Jenny even knew that I fell for her, I never told her, and anyway she told me that she fancied Paul Burbridge, and I certainly couldn't compete with him.

I did see her from time to time at Oxford. And our two college C.U.s (she was at St Hugh's) had a joint picnic one summer's evening by the river, which included some punting; and I was looking forward to this for weeks because I thought she'd be going.

Of course it was unrequited love, and I never saw her or heard from her again after she left Oxford.

Paul Burbridge (mentioned above – he was who Jenny liked) was the leader of our college C.U. during my first year. He was then in the second year, and he was the most charismatic person in the C.U. He was studying English, and not only was very good at that (he was to get a first), but was greatly talented in many other ways. For instance, he was an excellent actor and singer, and played the guitar too (and even wrote songs).

The college (as opposed to the university) had a kind of union. This was the Junior Common Room (JCR) which elected a leader every year, and there were other posts too which were elected. There were meetings held every so often, and motions passed, but I don't really remember it being very rebellious at all.

One thing I do remember (which was just a bit rebellious I suppose), was that the college union leader was caught with a girl in his room one night (i.e. staying the night) which was against college rules. He was fined, and at the next meeting the JCR voted to pay his fine.

When I had my voice problem, starting around Easter in my second year in the sixth form, obviously I was sent to a consultant – an ear, nose and throat specialist. He said there was nothing physically wrong with me, but that the problem was due to overwork.

Looking back, this 'diagnosis' now makes me angry for a number of reasons. Because of him saying that, when I went to university I went to the other extreme. Because I was so worried that if I worked hard I would lose my voice again, I did hardly any work at Oxford at all. And during one of my first weeks there, I was in a conversation where a second year student said he found he preferred to read books rather than go to lectures. There were some students who had that opinion (and it wasn't compulsory to go to lectures), but I think they were nearly all 'arts' students (English, history, etc). For science and mathematics it really was pretty bad advice. But I lapped it up and in fact went to very few lectures. And the trouble was I didn't put much effort into reading books either. I suppose I must have averaged quite a bit less than one and a half hours work a day, in total, which was a ridiculously low amount.

Most students at Oxford at that time in fact worked very hard. Many of my friends were putting in over 10 hours a day. My 2 best friends (Martin Liebeck and Dan Hastings) – both doing maths and both in the Christian union – worked between 10 and 12 hours most days, and then continued to work hard (at maths) during vacations. They both became professors, by the way, having got very good firsts (I think everyone was told, in those days, exactly what position they came out of those that got firsts – I'm not sure if they still are). (And incidentally, although I had worked quite hard when in my second year in the sixth form, it wasn't anything like that – it was never really more than about 7 hours a day – 5 hours at school and about 2 hours homework most evenings.)

It was ridiculous, at Oxford, really – I would find any excuse not to do work – walking into town or going to see one friend after another for coffee until all the day was taken up – and there was generally something to do in the evening.

Anyway, of course, because of that I got the inevitable third, and that really proved a disadvantage to me. I wasn't able to get a job in the fields I was attracted to, but instead went into computing, which I didn't fancy at all. My instincts must have been trustworthy, because I had no aptitude in that direction and hated it right from the start. After a few very stressful years doing this job I hated, I resigned from it all of a sudden, and took a job – and not a particularly good job – in sales. And it was some considerable time before I got myself 'sorted out' in that direction.

It makes me angry with the NHS because if the specialist had said the problem was, say, 'stress' (rather than 'overwork') I probably wouldn't have had that reaction, and wasted all those years.

One student who I remember particularly, who was a real intellectual, was Chris Jones. He was a year above me and studying PPE (philosophy, politics and economics). He was one of the very few people I ever knew who could talk intelligently about a book (or books) he had read, presumably only once, for ages and ages. Maybe that ability was more common than I realised, but I mixed mainly with maths students and it was certainly uncommon among them.

I remember Chris Jones coming to visit me and saying that he found me difficult to understand

– I think it was common knowledge how little work I did and he couldn't understand that. (Of course, I had my reasons, which I've already told you about, but I didn't broadcast those while I was at college – I don't think I told anybody.)

Chris Jones, who I think got a first in PPE, must have gone on to study theology, because he became ordained and then returned to St Peter's College as the Chaplain (which meant he taught theology to theology students too – he would have been a Fellow (teacher) of the college, not just Chaplain).

Apart from the college Christian union, which every college had, there was a joint university-wide Christian union (OICCU – Oxford inter-collegiate Christian union) which had meetings every Saturday and Sunday evening, which a large number of students attended. They had a different speaker each weekend who would usually do both. On the Saturday it would be a Bible study and on Sunday an evangelistic address, to which you were expected to invite your unconverted friends. Very often he (it was very rarely a woman) would be quite famous in Christian circles.

For example, one time it was David Watson, vicar of a church in York, who had written many books, and was very well-known. I didn't enjoy the address very much, it was very much a 'fire and brimstone' speech which put me off going much more after that, in fact. However, he was very popular with many of the students. Speakers who tended to go on about hell and damnation were called 'chunky' by CU students, and it was usually meant as a compliment. Paul Burbridge went to work in David Watson's church in York, forming the church theatre group 'Riding Lights' which toured the country's churches, putting on performances – many evangelistic in theme, I believe.

David Watson was to die quite young, of cancer, not very many years later.

In my first year I got involved with the college rowing club for a couple of terms. This was my first taste of seeing 'real keenness'.

We had to get up at 6, for a practice starting at 7am (and remember, we *were* students!) I cannot now remember how many days a week this was – I think it was quite a few, though.

We were instructed in all the techniques of how to handle our oar, including how not to 'catch a crab' (that's when you nearly pull the boat over). The coach – who would be a much more experienced second or third year student – would ride along by the river bank on his bike, megaphone in hand, yelling instructions and getting much more excited about it all than I ever managed to do.

The other student who had come to St Peter's from my old school (John Hanson School) at the same time, Nick Goddard, became much keener on rowing than me. I think he kept up his involvement throughout his 4 years at St Peter's (he studied chemistry, which was a 4 year course). Because of his very slight build he became the cox of the main college boat.

Some rowers in the college were ridiculously dedicated – for instance spending 5 or 6 hours a day on the water, in a totally futile attempt to get into the Blues squad – futile because the ones I am thinking of were completely the wrong physique – tall and quite skinny.

I told you I got involved with St Aldate's Church. It certainly took seriously the fact that it had a big student 'population' – and during every vacation it had something lined up for these students.

During the Christmas and Easter vacations there were stays for between a few days, and a week or so at Christian retreats. I remember one in Sunbury run by the Salvation Army and another in Devon called Lee Abbey. At each of these there would be a full programme of Christian teaching – the evangelical variety, of course – given by the vicar and curates of St Aldate's.

At Lee Abbey we students had to work very hard on jobs on the estate every morning for about 4 hours – it was quite a hard graft. With the teaching as well there wasn't all that much time to do as one pleased.

I remember one occasion, however, when we did have some free time. There was a piano in the large lounge (guess what that mainly was used for!) and I was with a group of students, one of whom was a good pianist. He started playing the piano and soon he was playing some pop music. About 5 or 6 of us students were standing round the piano and started singing along to this pop music. I remember I found it very pleasurable. It wasn't for long though. Within about 10 minutes others in the lounge had complained (there weren't just students there) and we were asked to stop. If we were going to use the piano it had to be for religious songs, we were told.

In my third year I had a room in one of the college-owned houses which were outside of the college, but still near the centre of Oxford. One of those who also had a room in the same house was Steve, who was reading physics.

Those who were doing physics, and some other sciences (and engineering), not only had lectures and tutorials to go to, like everyone else, but many hours of practicals each week too, in the laboratories. I'm sure they drew the short straw in that they had to put in many more hours to get an equivalently good degree.

Mathematics was the only subject where you didn't have to write essays, so even Steve, with his practicals to attend, had to write an essay each week.

And he had a regular routine. During most of the week he would prepare most of the facts and ideas for his essay – do the necessary reading etc. And the night before his tutorial, every week he would be up literally all night writing it. He showed me a couple and they were 20-25 pages long. I believe he would have been drinking quite a few cups of coffee on those Wednesday nights.

Most days we would go to the college buttery for lunch, in the years we weren't living in college. It didn't really have a very wide selection of food, but there were large portions. One of my regular meals was veal and ham pie (quite a massive slab) and baked beans. The buttery also served beer, but I only very occasionally had that. I don't think anyone I knew in the CU drank alcohol much at all (or smoked) and I was no exception. The only time was when a few of us went to a nearby pub, the Nag's Head, for a meal – usually steak – and we would have a pint with that. Being in the CU I certainly missed out on all the excessive (or even moderate) drinking and drug-taking –

that was another world.

Oxford had a much stronger Christian union than most other universities (in numerical terms). I think it was because so many students came from public schools which would have Christian unions – whereas state schools generally didn't have them.

And St Peter's in particular had a strong evangelical tradition because it had started out as an ordination college.

Anyway, it meant that college CU meetings were very well attended. There would sometimes be about 30 students at them (out of a college population of about 300).

There was a Bible study meeting every week. They would of course be held in the evening, and a meal would be laid on. I was sometimes responsible for getting the food for this – and usually several loaves of crusty bread, quite a bit of cheese, jars of Branston Pickle and pickled onions, maybe tomatoes and celery would be purchased. Each student attending would contribute towards the cost of this meal, of course.

There would be themes to the Bible studies and we'd generally 'cover' about one chapter in an evening – perhaps a whole term devoted to one of St Paul's letters, for instance.

The evening meal in college was quite a posh do. It was waiter service (as for all meals in college). Also you had to wear your gown. If you were a scholar you would have a long gown. Exhibitioners and commoners wore shorter gowns. (At your admission to the college it was decided whether you were a scholar, exhibitioner or commoner – it depended mostly on your entrance exams and interview(s) – scholar was the best, exhibitioner second best.)

The meal would be at 7.15. Grace was said in Latin, by one of the students (on a rota). Usually it was quite short, but once a week there would be a long one. The dining hall was quite dark inside – it reminded me a bit of a church. There were three long tables running lengthways for the students and one table (crossways) for the dons. They would be drinking wine with their meal. I will say that the food was quite healthy – it wasn't chips with everything and lots of burgers, like it would soon become in most educational establishments – and perhaps already was, in quite a few.

Even if you were not living in college, you were required to go to quite a few evening meals in college each term. Everyone lived in college during their first year, but St Peter's was short of accommodation, so only a minority of second and third year students lived in.

I never went to the Oxford union to a debate. I wasn't interested that much in politics, although I had been quite interested when in the sixth form. (After I became religious I wasn't that interested in anything, to be frank.) I suppose I leaned to the left if anything. Actually, it was only a minority who ever did go to the Oxford union debates, I think. For one thing there was quite a large membership fee for the union.

There was another reason, besides me working less than one and a half hours a day, why it was practically a miracle that I even got a third.

Doing a mathematics degree is not really one long plod lasting three years! It is divided up into a lot of quite separate subjects. For example, there is analysis, statistics, electromagnetic theory, Galois theory, group theory… in fact very many that bear little relation to each other.

We would normally study two of these subjects at a time, for about 4 – 6 weeks, before moving on to another two subjects (there would be two tutorials a week). Each of these subjects would be tested in the final exams. Now, about the first third of the work for each subject was generally 'introductory stuff', which would not be tested in the exams – it might typically be the first 4 or 5 chapters of the book we were reading on that subject. It was only when you had passed this introductory stage that you got onto the work about which there would be questions. So, with me doing so little work, I would find that I would start a new subject, just about manage to do the introductory stuff in my allotted 4 weeks (which was supposed to be done in 2 weeks) and then the tutor would tell me to start with a new subject, so it seemed I rarely ever got onto work that was actually tested in the exams.

My best friend throughout my three years at St Peter's was Martin Liebeck. (He was one of the two students who had 'evangelised' me when I first went up to Oxford.) His father was a 'Reader' in mathematics at Keele University. (Reader is just one grade lower than Professor.) And his mother was a lecturer in mathematics at a teacher training college near Stoke-on-Trent. He had two sisters, one of whom did a degree in mathematics as well, so it was a very mathematical family! I did actually meet them once, because I went on a fortnight's holiday with Martin during a vacation and we went to his place at the end of it. They were very pleasant, though I doubt that I gave a very good impression, not least because my razor had broken a few days before the end of the holiday (I used an electric razor), so I was unshaven for a few days when I met them.

Anyway, Martin worked very hard at his maths (over 10 hours a day, usually, I think), but certainly got the results, with a first and going on to get a PhD and become an academic. By the time he was in his mid-thirties, he was a professor, I believe. But despite working hard, he found time for many other pursuits, and was good at most of them.

He was excellent at cricket, playing most weeks during the season for the college team and very often scoring 70 or 80 runs. He was a very good musician too and played viola in a college or university chamber orchestra. And he was also good at squash and tennis (and chess).

One thing he wasn't quite so good at was football – I was about as good as him at that and we both played for the college 2nd team. I was quite enthusiastic about our football, but a high percentage of games were cancelled, which was always disappointing. This was because the groundsman always gave the first team priority – if the ground was waterlogged obviously neither team played, but if it was quite wet usually the first team played and the second didn't.

From all this you can see that I was overshadowed a bit by Martin Liebeck. I had been very good at a few things, especially in the few years before going to Oxford, but it perhaps didn't show when I was there. For instance, I had been good at singing (I sang in a choir at Andover for about 4 years), but obviously with my voice problem I couldn't do that at all – (I could speak alright after my first Christmas vacation, as stated earlier, but things like giving speeches or singing were not on). And I had been good at sailing – I helped my father build a Mirror dinghy when I was 14 and sailed that quite a bit (we added an Enterprise dinghy a couple of years later). This was in Pagham in West Sussex where my parents owned a caravan. But I never did any sailing connected with the university, even though they did have a sailing club.

Two of the other maths students in my year were Les Sheppard and Trevor Ward, both of whom I met recently at a reunion. Trevor was very good at tennis (even better than Martin Liebeck – he was no. 1 in the college, I believe). He became a Commander in the navy. And I remember that Les had an ambition as a student to go into computing, and he must have liked it a *lot* more than me, because he still works for a software house.

Almost everyone at the university went punting on the river, I think. Of those I knew, Dan Hastings was the most enthusiastic. He was very keen on the ladies, too, and I'm sure the two keenesses went together, for there was nothing more romantic than taking a young lady punting.

The river passed through the university parks, and added pleasure was to be had by taking a picnic and disembarking there for an hour or so for lunch or dinner.

Further down the river was a stretch called Parsons' Pleasure, where ladies were expected to disembark and walk round and rejoin the punt later, because in that bit of river there would be men – the parsons, or more likely, academics, swimming there naked. This was a tradition going back hundreds of years, I believe.

I had a letter from a girl I had fancied at school, who wrote that she, with her boyfriend, had gone to Oxford for the day, tried the punting, and that she had disobeyed the order to disembark at that point – had laid down flat in the boat, in fact, as I'm sure was common. And she described seeing all these middle-aged men, of all shapes and sizes, in the river and on the river bank, as naked as the day they were born.

Occasionally St Peter's CU would have a joint punt party with the CU of one of the women's colleges, of an evening. Together with the picnic on the river bank, about 3 enjoyable hours would be spent in this way. I looked forward to these events, because it wasn't that often I got to spend much time with girls.

Unlike in most colleges, and most subjects, we mathematicians at St Peter's of that time weren't tested at all between the end of the first year, and just before finals at the end of the third year. I think Martin Powell (my main tutor) got a shock as to how little I knew about what was to be tested in finals, when did finally have a 'collection' about 6 weeks before finals. ('Collections' were unofficial college exams.) He told me I might actually fail.

Quite a number of the students in the college CU I would classify as 'very keen indeed'. (I did not really count myself among that number.) For them, the *only* thing that really mattered was getting other students (i.e. 'non-Christians') interested in Christianity. So at the fellowship meetings, there would sometimes be quite a few comments about conversations CU students had had with 'non-Christians', and how they had angled the conversation to bring up the subject of Christianity – usually hoping for an opportunity to invite these people to the next Sunday evening OICCU evangelistic address.

In the Christian bookshops there would be books with titles like 'How to convert your friends'. When, years later, I became a salesman, I noticed that there were quite a few similarities between the books on selling ('Closing the sale', etc) – and these 'how to evangelise' books I had come across earlier. (Not that I was ever much of an 'evangelist' myself). (I read quite a few Christian books – it was just another way to avoid doing any work – but I must admit I put hardly any of it (the suggestions) into practice – even when it came to that I was extremely lazy.)

For many CU students, being a missionary was the most revered work you could possibly aspire to. In fact I can recall that we received teaching that seemed to imply that not becoming a missionary would be a sin. (However, when it came to actually looking for a job, only quite a small percentage of CU students became missionaries – it was much more common to go into banking or accountancy!)

My one and only girlfriend who was a fellow student was a girl called Heather. It happened in my third year, and we met at a disco organised by St Catherine's College. She was studying English at St Hilda's college, and was a year below me. She worked much harder than me – harder than average, in fact – and I believe she got a first and then embarked on a high-flying career in the Civil Service, with accelerated promotion.

She was very attractive and had long fair hair – was more or less a blond, in fact.

I visited her often in her room at St Hilda's (and sometimes some of her girlfriends would be there, so I met them too – I quite enjoyed that, being the only man amongst a group of 6 or 7 girls!).

Our relationship didn't last that long, though she did come to visit me in Andover during the Christmas vacation, and came to my 21st birthday party.

By the time I left Oxford, after 3 years, my interest in Christianity – or certainly my enthusiasm – was beginning to wane. I remember, during Eights week (a sort of festival, connected with the rowing club, during the summer term), seeing Michael Green (the vicar at St Aldate's), talking evangelistically in a marquee, trying to make the crowd interested in what he was saying, and I was thinking that he really looked a bit ridiculous.

One thing that was quite amusing, looking back, was CU members' definition of a 'lively church'. Quite often, in a conversation, you would hear someone describe a church as a lively church. I soon realised that all this in fact meant was that the church had quite a number of young people in its congregation. So that, if a church in a university town, say, managed to attract a fair number of students, it was a 'lively church'. But one that had mainly middle-aged or elderly people in the congregation was a 'dead church'.

A lot of Oxford colleges had quite famous Masters. I think to be offered a Mastership of an Oxford college towards the end of one's working life was regarded as an honour rather like getting a knighthood. Our Master was Sir Alec Cairncross, a famous (and politically left-leaning) economist who had advised several leaders of the Labour party.

(I think these days this practice has gone by the wayside a bit – and the Master is likely to be a younger person who has risen through the ranks of academia.)

There would be about 9 or 10 students doing maths each year at the college, so about 30 in all three years, and there were two mathematics tutors. Generally tutorials had two students, and we would have two tutorials a week. So, working it out, I suppose this aspect of their work would take up about 15 hours of each tutor's time each week during term time – certainly quite a lot. Oxford is very proud of its tutorial system.

BONUS SECTION III

'Making The Most Of Our Opportunities' & 'Generally Giving A Good Impression'

Quite a few of the following articles are written with a male readership in mind, but in fact most of them (apart from the first two) are relevant to both sexes.

Article 3.1

About clothes I

Obviously, the clothes a man wears is one of the ways he impresses people (or otherwise). (It's something that is on a par with our conversation skills in importance, in my opinion.)

I'll just say a few things about this.

Firstly, for most men I'd say wear casual, rather than very formal clothes where possible. Ditch that suit and tie! (You don't want to look like an accountant.)

A lot of men (myself included) haven't really got naturally great taste in choosing clothes that suit them. So here are a few tips if you come in to that category.

1) The Sales Trick

Go into a menswear shop that has a "selective" sale – "15% off everything" is no good. You need one where some clothes are reduced by 40-45%, say – and others not at all.

Then, unlike everyone else, choose what to buy from the clothes that <u>aren't reduced.</u>

The reasoning.

In a selective sale, the slow moving items are what are normally reduced – the things they can sell easily anyway are the ones that aren't (reduced). And in clothes choice anyway, I believe democracy "works". That is, you're better off sticking to the fast moving stock.

2) Follow that Man

Assuming you're male, and heterosexual, don't spend all your time at the pubs and clubs looking at the girls. Observe the men too.

Occasionally you'll notice someone dressed quite a bit better (in your opinion anyway) than the others. Take a note of what he is wearing (preferably on a scrap of paper or something – your memory might fail you the next morning – particularly if you're on your third pint, and there's four more to come!).

Then, the following weekend, go round the clothes shops in a good shopping centre, and choose more or less the same outfit as the man you thought looked pretty good. It doesn't have to be exactly the same make and everything – but the same colour and the same sort of style. (It helps anyway when you know what you're looking for, when you go into a clothes shop.)

[And the fact that you've seen it worn is much better than trying to decide from a row of shirts (or whatever) on hangers.]

Tip: if you live in a smallish town, probably best to do your "observing" in another, larger town or city.

3) Not the Cheapest

Whilst I don't see any point really in spending a fortune on individual items of clothing (£150-£200 on a pair of trousers, say), neither is it usually good to go for the very cheapest. Using the same example, I'd probably go for the trousers (or jeans) I liked best in the £30 - £40 range – a little, but not too much, above the average price.

4) Jewellery

When I bought a bracelet for about £50 – after having not worn any jewellery at all, except a watch, for years – I couldn't believe how many people mentioned about it. I'd recommend always wearing (at least) one item of jewellery, apart from a watch (again, not too cheap).

Article 3.2

About Clothes II

This was written several years ago.

This is something else I would like to say relating to men's choice of clothes.

For several years I really lost interest in all aspects of fashion – being broke most of the time didn't help.

But about a year ago, I started to regain an interest much more, in how I dressed. I found myself with a bit of spare money, and went round a few clothes shops, and chose some things I liked.

Amongst these were a couple of items in green – some mid-green trousers (or perhaps more towards a darker green), and a jacket that was a different, lighter shade. Both, I thought, looked pretty cool.

Though, as I say, I had no interest in fashion for quite a few years, and didn't know what "the scene" was, these days.

Anyway, I was wearing one or other of these items - I think the trousers, in one of the pubs I went to, and there was a comment from someone sitting down behind me (I was standing at the bar), - effectively he was wondering, he said, if I was gay – obviously because of the clothes I was wearing.

I must admit I was very disconcerted about this. I started to think that perhaps green was now the "trademark colour" that gays wore, or something like that.

For a few months I didn't wear green anymore.

But just recently, I have re-thought this.

I have noticed for a long time that most men

took very little interest in the clothes they wore – or at least that is how it appeared to me. The main colours worn seemed to be black, browns and blues – very little else. Also many of the clothes you saw men wearing seemed to be ill-fitting and very well worn.

And it has suddenly occurred to me that gays are now thought to have a <u>monopoly</u> on dressing well. That is, if you take an interest in what you wear at all, in some circles it is now assumed you must be gay.

And I believe this is a sorry state we have reached.

And I've revised my decision not to wear green clothes hardly at all, too – for the following reason.

When you think about it, men don't really have too many options when it comes to colour.

Red is mostly inappropriate, and in my opinion anyway, browns can be a bit staid and boring

– usually making you look older (than other colours). And I feel blues have been quite a bit too common for years – especially with nearly everyone wearing fairly standard blue jeans such a lot of the time.

And if you then decide that green is a no-go area, you begin to be very restricted.

So I'm now prepared to take the flak, if necessary. I'll choose the clothes I think look good, and if people want to insinuate anything from that, that's up to them.

The good news is that women seem to have much more sense – it is only men who have this attitude. I've found that women take more interest in you if you wear clothes that stand out, not less. Certainly it's not a good idea to wear all pastel colours from heat to foot, for instance – or something obviously effeminate (assuming you're heterosexual), but apart from that, I think wearing something that stands out is, as I say, a plus point.

And yes, I have found, as it happens, that

some of the best looking jackets I've seen, for example – and two of which I've been bought recently – have been various shades of green.

And if a few weirdos want to start saying things because of that, that's tough – as long as it's just men who have that attitude, it really doesn't bother me.

The next few articles are about how to impress others with your home.

Article 3.3

The Bathroom

Starting with the bathroom, then. Firstly I would recommend going upmarket with your choice of towels – spend twice as much as average on these and it can give a very good impression indeed. Likewise bath and toilet mats. Also invest in good quality fittings e.g. towel rails or whatever.

But one thing I would also recommend is to have a "proper" (power) shower – rather than just the fitting on the end of a rubber tube that you put on the taps.

You do not have to spend a fortune on this. There is a very nice "Triton" one you can get from Argos for about £130, for instance.

All these are things you can afford without having a well paid job, but they'll give the impression that you do.

Article 3.4

Be A Little Dim

One thing I would strongly recommend, is to have a light dimmer switch in your living room. I think it is quite romantic, when with a girlfriend, to be able to vary the light, from quite dark to bright, depending on our mood.

These dimmer switches are not new. I remember my uncle had one, and was very proud of it, over 30 years ago. I am really surprised that they haven't become much more popular – really I am surprised that it is not the case that just about everyone has one – but it isn't.

A very high percentage of restaurants have made use of subdued lighting to add romanticism for very many years, and there is no doubt that it has an effect.

Because of the fact that relatively few people have them, I believe they still have the power to impress as "a bit of a gadget" too.

And they are actually very cheap – about £10. Of course, if you can't fit it yourself, you will probably have to pay an electrician to do so.

Article 3.5

Get A Few "Small Luxuries"

* This article also was written a few years ago.

When people start thinking of spending money on the home, often their thoughts turn immediately to the BIG things. That new kitchen at £15 000, or expensive new furniture for the lounge.

And then, these same people may well scrimp and save when it comes to towels for the bathroom, or lightshades (whereas I've recommended you don't).

Now I'm going to suggest that you forget about those big things for now, but that you allocate maybe £1000 on what I'd call "small luxuries".

To give an example.

I can't be the only person who finds ordinary instant coffee (even supposedly good brands) not a very nice drink at all, but loves an occasional cup of filtered or percolated coffee.

So – buy a decent coffee percolator for a start – it will give a very good impression when you are able to offer "real" coffee to your guests.

I went round my nearest Debenhams and listed things I saw that one might buy with this £1000...

The first thing that caught my eye were a variety of expensive looking glasses, but which were all actually quite reasonably priced – no more than 4 for £15. There were champagne glasses, hi-ball glasses, wine and whisky ones – take your choice.

Staying with the subject of drink, there were cocktail shakers for £15.

Moving on to what one might find in the kitchen, there were a wide selection of goodies…

12 inch non stick wok set £20

Brito water filter £19

Arden professional oven to table casserole £53

George Foreman lean mean fat grilling machine £60

Breville toasted sandwich press £30

Morphy Richards Cafe Rico Filter Coffee maker £25

Juice making machine £40 (Kenwood) or £50 (Moulinex)

Posh kettle (Prestige) £30

Prestige toaster £25

Luxury stainless steel litter bin £75

Even if you treated yourself to 8 of these things, it probably wouldn't cost more than £350.

You get the idea. And if I had my £1000 in my pocket I probably would be tempted to spend some of the rest on some crockery – a relatively expensive make, for instance Denby.

Article 3.6

Buy A "Home Office" Cabinet

I recommend that you buy a lockable "home office" cabinet that you can get from any office equipment and stationary store for twenty odd pounds.

One of the things we don't want to do is to leave sundry papers lying around when we have visitors. It is also not good to bung all these papers in the nearest drawer half an hour before our visitor is due to arrive.

It is for this reason that we need a properly organised "home office system" with a proper place for each type of correspondence etc, that we take some effort to stick to. It will save time in the long run, because if we use the aforementioned "stick in the nearest drawer" method, it can take hours afterwards to find the particular piece of paper we want – sometimes even we may never find it, or it can get thrown away.

Allocate maybe an hour a month to go through all your papers in the home office to see if there's anything outstanding you've forgotten that needs to be done.

Equally important is to throw papers etc away that don't need to be kept. There is no point in having 10 times as much correspondence as we really need, and anyway these home office cabinets are very limited in space.

Things like bank statements, of course, should be kept, because there are occasions when these are required, and it it expensive to obtain copies. Utility bills too, are often required as proof of address, so don't throw all these away.

On the other hand, we can't expect to keep "everything sorted" exactly as we'd like it all the time, continuously.

I personally find it quite stressful to continuously keep the place presentable just in case someone visits at any time – that can turn into a full time job, almost.

So I far prefer to know when I'm going to have visitors just so I can give the place the once over half an hour before they come. I hardly ever have visitors arrive "on the off-chance".

Article 3.7

Don't Be Too Extravagant

I would say, to give the best impression, even if you have a well paid job, it's best to show in some areas at least, a very definite <u>lack of extravagance.</u>

That is to say, you don't want to have the latest of everything, even in the unlikely event that you could afford it. If everything in your home seems to be no more than a couple of years old, I believe you won't be giving such a good impression as you might think. (She'll probably think you owe about 15 grand to the credit card companies for a start.)

Although in some areas, I would suggest you go a bit upmarket (I've already mentioned towels in the bathroom – lightshades is another thing I would spend a little bit more on perhaps – everyone can afford to be a bit extravagant on these sort of things which don't cost much anyway) – but there's a case for going in the opposite direction in other areas.

For example, most of my relatives seem to go for very expensive carpets - £40 a sq metre or so – that sort of thing. I happen to think that that is totally unnecessary. You can get quite good carpet for bedrooms for about £6 a sq m, or for living rooms for £8 or £9* a sq m. There's really no need to pay more.

Anyway, just remember – that obviously second hand dining room suite may be the reason she decided she will, after all, see you again!

this article was written several years ago, and these prices might be a bit out of date now

Article 3.8

Lessons From Ms Arsan

(Here, I am assuming a male reader, but it's equally valid for women, I believe.)

In the famous film Emmanuelle, one of the messages the author (of the original book), Emmanuelle Arsan, seems to give is that the best sex is not between 2, but 3. (Though I'll not attempt to describe the plot – anyway I think the film is still available on DVD.)

I don't think the author means 3 in a bed sex or anything like that (it doesn't mean it in that literal sense in the film, by the way). But certainly the idea of "the best sex is for 3" seems to be a bit of a lynchpin.

(Incidentally, this article is about initially getting to know a girl through conversation – not the physical side at all.)

First of all, I'll put forward another idea that almost became an article - "Conversation in certain circumstances is sex". Okay it never made it past the "gatekeeper", but there is something about it that is quite meaningful to me.

And I've suddenly recalled a "pattern" - that often things have gone much better with a woman – at least from the point of view of giving a good first impression (I'm pretty sure) when I was part of a group of 3 – another man, me and the woman (or occasionally me and 2 women).

I believe that when a man "chats up" a girl, however skilful a conversationalist he is, however much he really likes her and is not just after "what he thinks might be able to get", it is all a bit too intense if there are just the two – almost inevitably.

But when there are 3 of you in the conversation – and preferably the other man is not "in competition", then everything is much less intense, which is much better.

A lot of the time you will be talking to the man, but of course the girl will overhear what you say, and you will still be impressing her. I will repeat, because it is a very important point – it is much less intense than if you were 100% talking to the girl.

Also the girl will want to know that you are able to get on well with men, as well as having charm enough for women to find you attractive.

Article 3.9

About "Looking For A Sign"

Quite a number of years ago. I went through a "religious phase". At the church I went to, it was quite common for the people to "ask God" (i.e. pray) for a "sign" about various things. One of the main ones was "who was the right person for them" i.e. who to marry.

I have to admit that I did this – it seemed like a good idea – since my relationships with girls didn't seem to last very long at this time.

And, yes, I did seem to have very clear "signs" that one girl, in particular, was "right for me". And I did manage to become quite close friends with her, in a way – though it must have been quite obvious, to anyone who knew us both, that we absolutely weren't suited to be married to each other.

In other words, these "signs" were very much

a mistake.

I do believe – though I may be wrong – that it is becoming even more common to "look for a sign" in this sort of way, even for non-religious people.

I would just like to make this comment.

People do have "signs", which seem to be more than coincidences, but there is a reason why I would suggest that anyone who does, doesn't necessarily go "overboard" - just as with me, it may well be a mistake.

The reason is (I think) that I have come to believe that in many of us (perhaps even most of us) – even quite "normal" people – there is a certain amount of "masochism" - I won't say more than that.

And these "signs", mostly, I believe, "sort of" come from our unconscious – I suppose that is fairly clear.

What I'm saying is that because there is very likely a bit of "masochism" in a lot of us, this is why we cannot necessarily trust "signs" - they may well be leading us in the <u>wrong direction.</u>

So, whether it is a dream, or perhaps you've just decided that you must end that relationship, and then that night you have a really dreadful night, and feel quite ill the next morning (which some may take as a "sign" that they've just made the wrong decision, and so reverse it) – I would say "Be careful, that "sign" may well be leading you in the wrong direction."

Article 3.10

Really, Really Learning Something

As we go through life, we all make up our own "rules" of the game. We discover things that work, and things that don't. We become our own ongoing agony aunt, as it were.

Unusually, I have made it my job to write down as many of these "rules" as I could, as they were discovered. (Most people leave everything more or less in their unconscious, I believe.)

But I have discovered that there are two levels of learning these "rules".

There is the first stage, where we see the "pattern" and we say to ourselves "Yea, that makes sense, I shall have to watch out for that." (In my case, I may even write the article then.)

But as yet we haven't really "owned" the idea. If it's some sort of "advice" on how to live, some "warning" perhaps, we may still go against that advice, that warning.

We may do that once or twice more, or even several times maybe. And perhaps each time we will suffer as a result.

And after maybe the second, or the fourth, time we go against that advice or warning, and we've noticed that each time we've suffered – at this stage we accomplish the <u>second</u> stage of learning.

Our negative experiences have confirmed the rule to us. Now we say to ourselves "Yes, that bloody well is right, and there's no way I'm going to make that mistake again." - and <u>mean</u> it.

We know that should we live to be 100, we're jolly well not going to fall into that trap again. (Perhaps that's a slight exaggeration, but we know at least that it will be much less likely in future.)

We have now _really_ learnt the rule. Congratulations are in order. And there is strength to be gained from reaching this position.

Article 3.11

When You're Looking For A Job, Think Of The Perks

In my case, because I did well in my A-levels, I went to Oxford; later, because I had a maths degree I went into computing.

At Oxford while I was there, there was about a 5:1 ratio of men to women. There was also what they called a "town and gown split" - people from the university rarely mixed with everyone else in Oxford. The upshot of it was that it was actually quite difficult for male students there to find girlfriends – many male students didn't have a girlfriend the whole time they were there, even though, in some respects they were among the most eligible young men in the country – and quite a lot from very rich families too (a high percentage had been to public school).

Again, when I was in computing, there were far

more men than women. It wasn't quite as bad as for mechanical or electronic engineers – in that there were hardly any women – but still the ratio wasn't much different from at Oxford.

That was me.

Now I think of the landlady, Lee, at my local a while ago.. Her son became a hairdresser. (He is about the same age as me.) That is a profession that is looked down on, to some extent, considered low status – or it used to be anyway. In fact Lee's husband, who had been an RAF pilot, was apparently extremely upset when the son made this decision.

But Lee told me that this son had "a ridiculous number" of girlfriends – what she was saying made me quite envious in a way. The point was he had an ideal job, really, for chatting up women. Basically he had probably about a dozen women in his chair each day for half an hour or so each, who were really a captive audience. No wonder he scored.

So that is going from one extreme to the other,

jobwise, in that respect.

And I sometimes wonder if I was so clever to go to Oxford, for that reason alone.

I think if I had my time again, that 5:1 ratio would have put me off quite a bit. (It's changed now, at Oxford, by the way – most colleges accept both sexes.) Likewise with the career choice.

And come to think of it, surely for a normal heterosexual person, having a job where you very frequently come into contact with a lot of attractive people of the opposite sex is a big plus point. It is very common for certain things to be valued in financial terms apart from the wages e.g. you will be told that that company car is "worth" £5000 a year or whatever (and these days taxed heavily on that basis too).

But I'd put a high value on, as I said, having a job where you frequently come into contact with people you find attractive - if you're single, anyway.

The moral of this is – if you're lucky in this respect and have been offered a job with £2000 a year more or something, think twice if it means a deterioration from the above-mentioned point of view. Or, if you're thinking of a career change, don't just consider the money angle!

Article 3.12

Choose Hobbies That Are "Unisex"

This is a similar point, really, to what I said about your career (article 3.11).

You are presumably going to choose possibly about 2 interests to make your major hobbies, and I think it makes real sense to choose ones that appeal to both sexes.

Therefore if you are a man, don't make chess your hobby (for some reason hardly any women are interested in that), but I would recommend something like photography or sailing.

Both men and women enjoy these greatly and that person you meet will probably be really pleased if they find one (or both) of them are among your interests.

Of course, if you can afford your own boat

(and I'm not talking about a 30 foot yacht – just a sailing dinghy even, perhaps), and join a sailing club on the coast, a lot of people would jump at the chance of going with you – for this reason I'd recommend getting a boat that can be sailed by 2 or 3 people, not one that is very much a one person effort. (And for this same reason, I'd recommend "proper" sailing, rather than windsurfing, for instance.)

Printed in Great Britain
by Amazon